CRYPTOCURRENCY

A Clear and Simple Guide to Understand and Master Cryptocurrency

ALFORD BENSON

© Copyright 2018 by Alford Benson - All rights reserved.

The following Paperback is reproduced below with the goal of providing information that is as accurate and reliable as possible. Regardless, purchasing this eBook can be seen as consent to the fact that both the publisher and the author of this book are in no way experts on the topics discussed within and that any recommendations or suggestions that are made herein are for entertainment purposes only. Professionals should be consulted as needed prior to undertaking any of the action endorsed herein.

This declaration is deemed fair and valid by both the American Bar Association and the Committee of Publishers Association and is legally binding throughout the United States.

Furthermore, the transmission, duplication or reproduction of any of the following work including specific information will be considered an illegal act irrespective of if it is done electronically or in print. This extends to creating a secondary or tertiary copy of the work or a recorded copy and is only allowed with express written consent from the Publisher. All additional right reserved.

The information in the following pages is broadly considered to be a truthful and accurate account of facts and as such any inattention, use or misuse of the information in question by the reader will render any resulting actions solely under their purview. There are no scenarios in which the publisher or the original author of this work can be in any fashion deemed liable for any hardship or damages that may befall them after undertaking information described herein.

Additionally, the information in the following pages is intended only for informational purposes and should thus be thought of as universal. As befitting its nature, it is presented without assurance regarding its prolonged validity or interim quality. Trademarks that are mentioned are done without written consent and can in no way be considered an endorsement from the trademark holder.

CRYPTOCURRENCY

Acknowledgment

I would like to give heartful thanks to my dear friend and colleague Robert Buxton who provided carefully considered feedback and valuable comments. I also owe a very important debt to Arnold Trent whose opinions and information have helped me very much throughout the production of this content.

ALFORD BENSON

This book is dedicated to Barbara Johnson, for her kindness and devotion, and for her endless support when Mary was ill; her selflessness will always be remembered.

Table of Contents

Acknowledgment 5
Table of Contents 7
Introduction 9
Chapter 1 Defining Cryptocurrency 11
Chapter 2 The Mechanics of Cryptocurrency 23
Chapter 3 The History of Cryptocurrency 35
Chapter 4 Applications of Cryptocurrency 47
Chapter 5 Trading and Investing Cryptocurrency 59
Chapter 6 Legal Concerns 71
Chapter 7 Security Risks 83
Conclusion 95

ALFORD BENSON

INTRODUCTION

Thank you for purchasing and downloading Cryptocurrency: A Clear and Simple Guide to Understand and Master Cryptocurrency! In this book, you will find a complete guide to everything you need to know about getting involved in cryptocurrency. Even if you are not seeking to trade or invest, this text will provide you with ample information to explain the subject to your peers, write books and articles on cryptocurrency, and generally understand this new and exciting technology. A large number of topics will be covered throughout this book, and each topic is separated into seven chapters.

There is a world of information on cryptocurrency, and this book will cover the main ones in detail. The topics to be covered include defining the invention of cryptocurrency, explaining the underlying mechanics behind cryptocurrency, exploring the history of cryptocurrency, reviewing all the new and upcoming applications of the technology, a primer on getting involved with trading and investing cryptocoins, legal concerns facing cryptocurrency, and lastly the security risks involved with cryptocurrency. Each chapter includes an introduction that explains what will be covered and a conclusion section that covers all of the important topics discussed in that chapter.

We hope that you find this book to be a handy and complete compendium of all things cryptocurrency. Thanks again for taking the time to explore this text, and best of luck in future forays into cryptocurrency and cryptocoin trading and investing.

CHAPTER 1
DEFINING CRYPTOCURRENCY

Cryptocurrencies are a new and exciting invention that has evolved into a worldwide phenomenon. A cryptocurrency is not just a new type of digital currency, it is a new technology built on an innovation in computer science. To understand everything we need to know about cryptocurrency, we need to understand the core concepts. In this chapter, we will look at what makes up a cryptocurrency. We will examine the conditions required to consider something a cryptocurrency. We will also learn about blockchain - the technology cryptocurrencies are built on. Lastly, we'll look at the role of cryptography in securing cryptocurrency.

A researcher from the University of Finance and Administration in Prague named Jan Lansky wrote that a cryptocurrency is defined as a system that meets six distinct conditions. First, it must not rely on a central authority. It also must keep a complete record of the currency units and who owns them. A cryptocurrency must define when you can create new currency units, and outline the process by which the units are created and owned. Through the use of cryptography, each unit of currency must have proof of ownership. The cryptocurrency system must allow transactions that change ownership of cryptocurrency units. Lastly, if there are multiple instructions for changing ownership of the same unit, only one of them can be performed. Like the laws of physics of robotics, these conditions provide a guideline for creating and defining a cryptocurrency.

Cryptocurrencies are decentralized by nature. As outlined by Lansky, a cryptocurrency cannot rely on a central source of authority. The blockchain technology that cryptocurrencies are based on does not use a central server for transactions or record keeping. Instead, cryptocurrencies rely on a peer-to-peer network of computers with each user keeping a full record of the transaction on their machine. The digital currencies that were attempted before cryptocurrency relied on a third-party service or corporation, while cryptocurrencies themselves operate on what is called a distributed ledger. A distributed ledger is a network that keeps an updated record, in this case, transactions, on many different nodes, or users.

A cryptocurrency must also keep a complete record of every unit, including who owns each unit. In the blockchain, this is represented by transaction data. If you know the transaction history of every digital wallet involved in a cryptocurrency, you know where each and every unit is and who owns it. For example, a wallet address might have a transaction history of receiving 5 Bitcoins and sending 3. From this data, we can conclude that this wallet has 2 Bitcoins without the need to directly read the wallet data. The blockchain behind cryptocurrencies stores all transaction data in a format that can be read but not feasibly modified. The cryptographic time-stamp is what allows this.

For a system to be considered a cryptocurrency it needs to clearly define how the units of currency are created and who they go to. In the case of Bitcoin, new cryptocoin units are created when users verify transaction data by creating cryptographic hashes. This process is called mining. As a reward for verifying the encrypted transaction data, computers that carry out the mining are given new units of crypt coins. This is the process in which new Bitcoins come into the market. This is a parallel to natural resources that are mined and then used as currency.

A cryptocurrency system must allow transactions to occur that change the ownership of the units. This is built into the core of blockchain and Bitcoin. With a Bitcoin client, you can send and receive cryptocurrency units between addresses. The statement for these transactions is issued by the same network that proves the ownership of the cryptocurrency units. For example, you can send 20 Bitcoins from your address to another and the network would keep track of the transaction as well as who owns the cryptocoins. For a cryptocurrency to be considered as such, it must first fulfill this condition.

Lastly, there must be a condition for requested actions performed at the same time. A situation may arise in which the system receives requests to send the same unit of cryptocurrency to different places. In this situation, at least one of the orders must be fulfilled. Without this condition, orders that are entered simultaneously cannot be fulfilled. In the case of Bitcoin, if two orders for changing the ownership of one unit of cryptocurrency are entered at the same time, at least one order is fulfilled. This ensures double-spending and fraud cannot occur. This final condition is a measure that prevents exploitation of the cryptocurrency.

These are the six main conditions for a cryptocurrency. If a system meets all of these requirements, it can be considered to be a cryptocurrency. A digital currency is not necessarily a cryptocurrency, but a cryptocurrency is always a digital currency. In review: Decentralized, complete record of units, process of creation and ownership explained, proof of ownership, transactions, and a solution for when transactions are made on the same unit at the same time. If and only if a system fulfills these requirements is it a cryptocurrency. The model for these requirements is the original cryptocurrency, Bitcoin. We can consider Bitcoin to be the originator of cryptocurrencies in general.

Ownership of these currency units needs to be proven beyond all doubt for the system to be considered cryptocurrency. In the blockchain, this means encrypting the transaction data with a cryptographic hash. The cryptography that protects the timestamped data from being modified ensures that transaction records are never modified. This securing of the transaction data means every unit of cryptocurrency is accounted for in every address it is sent and received to. The digital wallets that hold the cryptocoins are written in the form of private keys, which are efficiently stored on the blockchain. For example, every Bitcoin created is accounted for by recording and securing every unit that is created, send, and received.

To understand the wide variety of cryptocurrencies out there, we must first understand the original cryptocurrency. The original cryptocurrency is known as Bitcoin. It is also the most popular variation of cryptocurrency. As the invention it is based on,

CRYPTOCURRENCY

Bitcoin is a metaphor for gold. It is mined like a natural resource, and over time more computing power is required to mine it. Just like gold, it has some practical use, but it ultimately used as currency for other goods and services. Unlike gold, it isn't physically mined. The process of cryptocurrency mining involves cryptographic math done on computers, but that will be covered later.

What gives a cryptocurrency value? Cryptocurrencies are usually represented as units of currency called cryptocoins. A single cryptocoin could be worth any amount of value in fiat currency. What gives the cryptocoin value is a community of people who use and accept it in exchange for goods and services. In the beginning stages of the first cryptocurrency, Bitcoin, it was worth between nothing a fraction of a cent in terms of US dollars. As the popularity of Bitcoin increased, so did the dollar value. Just as any other currency, a cryptocurrency gets value from the value people assign to it.

To understand what cryptocurrency is at its core, we must first understand blockchain technology. We will elaborate more on blockchain in the following chapter, but a rudimentary understanding is important to comprehend the basics of cryptocurrency. We will do this by describing the structure of the blockchain in more abstract terms. First, the blocks that make up a cryptocurrency network. Next, the "chains" that link these blocks together. While more intimate details build a deeper comprehension, having a basic idea of how the underlying structure works give a working idea. We will expand on this working idea shortly after covering the basics.

The "block" in a blockchain is a type of data structure. In the block is stored a variety of information in various types to build the structure of a cryptocurrency. This information includes network transaction data, a cryptographic hash of the previous block, an un-modifiable timestamp, identifying information, hashing difficulty, and more. Every user in a blockchain has access to these blocks, and they contain all of the necessary information for keeping track of who owns what cryptocoins and where they are sending them. Using cryptography, as will be expanded upon later in the chapter, these blocks of information are completely protected from any hacking or modification.

The "chain" that binds the blocks together into a blockchain is contained within the blocks themselves. As mentioned before, each block contains within it a cryptographic hash of the previous block. This is essentially the information of the last block encrypted into an indecipherable secret code stored in the current block. This is what binds the blocks together. All blocks contain cryptographic hashes of the last blocks, with the exception of the first block. For this reason, the first block is also known as the "genesis block." Including forks and other deviations, all blocks in the blockchain can be traced back to the genesis block.

Bringing these two elements together, we get a rudimentary picture of what the blockchain is. With a rudimentary picture of what the blockchain is, we have a workable understanding of how cryptocurrency works. Blocks are records of transaction information that contain within them important identifying data. One such piece of data is an encrypted hash of the last block's data. The chain is this connection of one block to the last by means of encrypted hashes. Together, we have a blockchain that is a sequence of transaction records secured and encrypted with cryptography. With these transaction records, we can see a complete picture of who has what cryptocoins and where they are being sent.

How do these cryptographic hashes work? So that we can grasp a cryptographic hash, we must first explore what cryptography is in the first place. The word cryptography comes from the Greek language and roughly means "hidden writing." The goal of cryptography is to change a message in such a way that it cannot be read by a third-party. Cryptography is used in cryptocurrency to secure data from being modified. In a cryptocurrency blockchain, the data is trusted and secure. This is because the cryptography securing the data is so strong that it is not feasible for anyone to be able to crack it. While theoretically possible, it is not feasible in real life to modify blockchain encrypted data. This is what makes cryptocurrency data reliable and secure.

Now that we know cryptography, what is a hash? A hash is a fixed amount of data produced from a hash function that takes an arbitrarily sized text string as an input. In computer science, a string is a type of data that stores text information. Much like a message in secret code, a hash is protected from reading by third parties by the complexity of its encryption. The hashes produced and stored in blocks are made from an algorithm that takes the previous block's transaction data as a string and turns it into a hash. Theoretically and practically, the hashes produced by the blockchains behind cryptocurrencies cannot be broken.

These are the essential ideas behind cryptocurrency. From these ideas, we can build a deeper understanding. We have learned the basic components of a cryptocurrency, and we have examined the conditions a system needs to be considered a proper cryptocurrency. We have briefly reviewed the blockchain, the technological foundation of cryptocurrency, and we have explored the essential precepts of the cryptography that makes a cryptocurrency work. The goal of these next chapters is to elaborate further on the mechanics, history, applications, trading, investing, legal concerns, and security risks of cryptocurrency. Consider this first chapter to a skeleton or primer on the subject and the following chapters as means to flesh out these ideas. Next, we will deeper into the mechanics of how a cryptocurrency works.

CHAPTER 2
THE MECHANICS OF CRYPTOCURRENCY

There is no denying that cryptocurrencies are complex systems. Even for investors and adopters, the mechanics behind a cryptocurrency can be confusing. With this chapter, we will walk through what makes a cryptocurrency tick. It's best to start from the ground-up and abstract basic ideas into the whole of cryptocurrency. The first thing we will do is dissect and take a detailed look at a block, the main component of a cryptocurrency's blockchain. After learning the structure of the block, we will take a look at how blocks are formed and then chained together with cryptography. After that comes learning about the distributed ledger, the network on which cryptocurrencies operate. Mining, the process by which new cryptocoins are created and distributed, will also be explained in detail. Wallets, the primary storage medium for cryptocurrency, will be elaborated on afterward. Lastly, we will cover the anonymity afforded by cryptocurrencies and how cryptocoins are moved between individuals and institutions.

What's in a block? A block is an abstraction of a data type in computer science called a "record." A record is similar to entries on a table. Each record in a blockchain such as the one behind Bitcoin contains a number of "fields." A field is like a column in this table. Each field is a specific type of data meant to serve a specific purpose. You can consider these records to be like pages in a book. Each page is linked to the next. In this case, the pages are linked by cryptographic hashes. In short, a block is a record of data fields. In the case of the blockchain, each record has five fields.

The five types of data in Bitcoin's blocks are a "magic number," blocksize, the blockheader, the transaction counter, and the transaction data. The magic number is a unique identifying number defining the block as a part of the network. The blocksize field defines exactly how large the block will be. The blockheader is a complex field that contains six fields within itself. The blockheader is likely the most important component of a block. The transaction counter is a number that keeps track of how many total transactions have occurred. Lastly, the transaction data is the actual information on what coins are being moved to which addresses.

To understand the blockheader, we must look at the six fields contained within it. These are the version, the hash of the previous block, the hash of the current block, the timestamp, the target, and the nonce number. The version indicates which version of software the block is operating in. The hash of the previous block, as explained earlier, is what links this block to the previous. The hash of the current block is stored in a similar manner directly after. The timestamp is a value, in seconds, that keeps track of when the data was last modified. An encrypted timestamp proves the information has not been tampered with. The target is a value that defines how difficult it is to verify the current block. Lastly, the nonce number is a value used by clients on the network to attempt to verify the hash.

When a new block is created, all of these values must be calculated by a computer. In the order listed, all values for the fields in the records are imported through calculation or reading of the previous block. This process of creating new blocks is at the core of cryptocurrency. For a cryptocoin to grow, new blocks must be constantly created and encrypted into the blockchain. The bulk of these block's information is made up of the transaction data occurring on the network. As we learned earlier, a complete and secure record of all transaction data gives a full picture of who owns which coins and where they are going.

Who creates these blocks? By the decentralized nature of the blockchain network, every user involved in a cryptocurrency has a hand in creating blocks. The processing power for the tasks involved in creating and linking new blocks is distributed across the users on the blockchain. In fact, the entire network is comprised of users connected to the blockchain. This peer-to-peer system is one of many measures in cryptocurrency that ensures there is no central authority or middle-man that can control or alter critical transaction information. This is the process by which new blocks are introduced into a cryptocurrency's blockchain.

The chaining of these blocks together is inherent in the process of creating new blocks. For a new block to be complete, the blockhead must contain a hash of the previous block. Any new block must be connected to the previous block in this manner. This process allows any user to view and read transaction data from blocks but prevents any user from tampering with or modifying the transaction data for illicit purposes. In this way, the chaining of blocks together in the blockchain creates data that is completely transparent, and it creates data that is feasibly impossible to hack or alter.

Why is this important? As we will expand upon soon, the process of chaining and verifying blocks creates new cryptocoins to distribute in the system. On top of that, creating a linked chain of blocks by encryption secures trust in the system. As we've mentioned, reversing the process of a cryptographic hash in a proper cryptocurrency system is practically impossible. With data from the previous blocks timestamped and turned into cryptographic hashes, no data in the whole network of cryptocurrency can be compromised. Without the process of chaining blocks together into a blockchain, the entire cryptocurrency system is not secure and subject to attacks or critical errors.

On what type of network are all these processes carried out? The network that blockchain, and therefore cryptocurrencies in general, are built upon is called a distributed ledger. This is a type of network that creates a consensus and synchronized collection of digital data across multiple networks.

Cryptocurrencies are built on a distributed ledger, and the data from the blockchain is shared through this distributed ledger. Each user in the network keeps the other accountable by having an identical, updated copy of the blockchain that everyone has. Let's take a look at the mechanics behind a distributed ledger in a cryptocurrency system.

In a distributed ledger, data is stored and verified across all users in the network. In a cryptocurrency system, the blockchain is stored across all clients. Whenever a change is made to the blockchain, users send updates to each other and verify any new changes. Without the need for a central server, all users on the distributed ledger maintain an identical, up-to-date version of the blockchain. The process by which this consensus is achieved is a mathematical algorithm called a consensus algorithm. Other than cryptocurrency systems like Bitcoin, there are a number of banks that employ the use of distributed ledgers to minimize risks.

Like any other currency system, new cryptocoins have to be created regularly. The process by which new cryptocoins are created is called mining. Mining involves adding onto the transaction records in the public ledger of the blockchain. Mining is done to maintain the distributed ledger of transaction data, but it also serves another purpose. To reward the user for performing the work of building the blockchain, units of cryptocurrency are rewarded to the miner each time a block is completed. In this way, mining Bitcoins is analogous to mining gold. As more and more Bitcoins are mined, it becomes more difficult to mine.

The difficulty of a mining operation is controlled by the previously mentioned field in a block's blockheader. This field can be referred as difficulty. The difficulty of mining increases as the blockchain grows. The reward given to miners also decreases over time. This limits the amount of total cryptocoins that can be mined. As with actual resources, it becomes more difficult over time to acquire more as the resource becomes depleted. This means that cryptocurrencies like Bitcoin often have a set limit as to how much units of cryptocoin can be mined. This scarcity of available cryptocoin units creates value.

You may be wondering how are these cryptocoins stored after being mined or traded. The solution for this is called a wallet. A wallet may refer to a collection of private keys to send and receive coins, but it may also refer to software that is designed to store units of cryptocurrency. Wallets can be hosted online or they can be operated as a desktop application. Many prefer to store their cryptocoins on desktop applications as it can be accessed while offline. There are many different forms of cryptocurrency wallets, and each one has advantages and disadvantages. Wallets are identified by a string of random characters called an address.

What kind of wallet should you use? First, consider the context in which you are using cryptocurrency. If you are using cryptocurrency for trading and investing, you may want to consider temporarily storing your coins online on exchanges specifically made for trading and investing. When not trading or investing, you generally want your cryptocoins in "cold storage." This means storing your cryptocurrency on a desktop application that can be accessed online or offline. When your cryptocoins are being stored online, there is the risk of not having access to your private keys or the online service shutting down unexpectedly. Similarly, if you are simply holding onto your cryptocurrency and not trading or investing, it is wisest to store your cryptocoins in cold storage on desktop wallet software. The original Bitcoin client comes with such wallet software, but there are different wallet programs for each type of cryptocurrency.

Addresses are identifiers usually between the range of 26 and 35 characters. When sending and receiving cryptocoins like Bitcoins, addresses are used as the destination. In this way, a cryptocurrency address is similar to a bank account number or routing number. Unlike account and routing numbers, a cryptocurrency address can only be used once. Fortunately, new addresses can be easily generated online or offline. As these random characters are not tied to any particular personal identity or institution, the process of sending and receiving cryptocurrency is anonymous by default. Cryptocurrency address cannot be used to identify any particular person or organization, and once they are used they need to be replaced by another randomly generated address. This anonymity combined with the security of the blockchain makes cryptocurrencies a reliable way to send and receive money.

This anonymity is very important to cryptocurrency in general. The intended purpose of the original blockchain based cryptocurrency, Bitcoin, was to provide a way for people and groups to send and receive money without the need for a third-party authority. In a cryptocurrency exchange, no personal or identifying information needs to be exchanged. In situations where security is paramount, the anonymity provided by cryptocoins is very useful. The exchange is performed exclusively between the two users involved, and the need for a financial institution to transfer money is eliminated. Without the need for a financial institution, there is no need to transfer anything other than the value involved in the trade.

In review, we have learned about the block and its importance in cryptocurrency and the blockchain structure. We also learned how a block is formed and then chained together through a unique cryptographic process. We have explored the idea behind the distributed ledger and the importance it has in cryptocurrency, and we have learned how the mining process work and the value it provides. On top of blockchain and distributed ledger, we dissected the idea of a cryptocoin wallet. We also analyzed what kind of cryptocoin wallets should be used in what contexts. Lastly, we analyzed the importance of the anonymity that cryptocurrency systems provide for users. It's time now have a look at the new and unique history behind cryptocurrency.

ALFORD BENSON

CHAPTER 3
THE HISTORY OF CRYPTOCURRENCY

Cryptocurrency carries with it a strange and fascinating history. In this chapter, we will break down the origins of cryptocurrency from early infancy in cryptographic research to the current state of the technology. The history of cryptocurrency at the time of this book's publication is not particularly long. The origins of cryptocurrency can be traced into the past over the span of roughly a handful of decades. We will look at the early science behind cryptocurrency, the release of Bitcoin and the mysterious figure behind it, the growth of Bitcoin, the development of additional cryptocoins, how competition works in cryptocurrency, and other critical points in cryptocurrency history.

The story of cryptocurrency begins in 1983 with a cryptographer named David Chaum. Chaum was a computer scientist who published the idea of a type of electronic, cryptographic currency system. He named this system "ecash." The idea of ecash was to build a system in which money could be withdrawn from a bank through software that required cryptographic keys. After submitting the proper cryptographic keys to the software, the user could send funds they've withdrawn. This system created a method of sending digital currency in a way that cannot be traced by a government, bank, or any other third party.

David Chaum would go on to carry out this idea through an invention called "DigiCash." DigiCash Inc. was formed in the year 1989 to carry out this proposed system of completely anonymous digital currency transactions. The transactions carried out to and from bank accounts through DigiCash required the knowledge of specific encrypted keys. Much like our modern cryptocurrency systems, DigiCash allowed users to transfer funds digitally between each other without the surveillance of banks or governments. The technology behind this system of anonymous digital money transfer was named "Blind Signature Technology." DigiCash was created out of concern surrounding the public nature of personal information and payment data online. DigiCash later declared bankruptcy in 1998 and was sold.

Seven years after the inception of David Chaum's digital cash system, a paper was published in 1996 titled, "How to Make a Mint: the Cryptography of Anonymous Electronic Cash" by the National Security Agency of the United States Department of Defense. This paper outlined the idea of electronic cash that was immune to communication eavesdropping. In this text are references and citations of the research done by David Chaum. The paper includes issues with digital cash that were later the focus of Bitcoin, like double-spending. This paper would go on take a new character many years later when the NSA's domestic spying program, PRISM, was revealed to the public.

In 1998 an idea for a distributed electronic cash system called "b-money" was proposed by cryptography writer and developer Wei Dei. An early predecessor to Bitcoin, "bit gold," was created by computer scientist Nick Szabo shortly after. Bit gold was another electronic cash system that revolved around cryptographic proof of work functions. This would later serve as the foundation for the cryptographic mining process of Bitcoin. As mentioned in the previously cited NSA paper, bit gold carried with it the issue of potential exploitation by double-spending. However, it would still be another decade before the first successful implementation would appear, Bitcoin.

In the year 2008, the idea of Bitcoin was proposed by an anonymous developer operating under the pseudonym, "Satoshi Nakamoto." Nakamoto is also responsible for creating the primary forum for Bitcoin discussion, Bitcointalk. To this day, there is uncertainty about who Satoshi Nakamoto really is. The creator of bit gold, Nick Szabo, denies that he is actually Satoshi Nakamoto, in spite of several attempts to prove otherwise using linguistics and circumstantial evidence. Not much is known about Satoshi Nakamoto. Many are not even sure that Satoshi Nakamoto is one person. Some suspect that Nakamoto may actually be a

group of people, while others suspect th
pseudonym used by Nick Szabo

A potential identity of Satoshi Nakamoto
named Dorian Prentice Satoshi Nakam
birth name is Satoshi Nakamoto, a
journalist Leah McGrath Goodman clai
was the Satoshi Nakamoto of Bitcoi
Nakamoto was a physicist and work
classified defense research projects. He h;
worked as a computer engineer for inforr
services in the finance industry. He claime
he worked on a project that had been turne(
to other people, like the Satoshi Nakamc
Bitcoin. In the interview following this, he d(
any connection to Bitcoin and pointed out th
had confused the question with his confide
work with the military.

Hal Finney stands as another possible invento
the blockchain. Finney was a pioneer
cryptography and the first person to use
blockchain software aside from Sato.
Nakamoto. Apparently, he also lived nearby to t
previously mentioned Satoshi Nakamoto. F
writing had been analyzed and proven to be ve1
similar to Satoshi Nakamoto's. It was speculate

one party to another without going through a financial institution ... The network timestamps transactions by hashing them into an ongoing chain of hash-based proof-of-work, forming a record that cannot be changed without redoing the proof-of-work." Satoshi Nakamoto's proposal was based on previous cryptographic hash signature chain research and was aimed at creating a viable electronic currency. The name, "Bitcoin," was strikingly similar to Nick Szabo's "bit gold." Unlike Nick Szabo's bit gold, Bitcoin solved the problem of double-spending with a record chained together by cryptographic hashes.

At first, bitcoin was not extremely popular. It would evolve later on to be a very popular digital currency but began as something between a handful of cryptography enthusiasts and developers. At this time, not many were aware of the potential of blockchain and cryptocurrencies, and it would be some years before major applications of blockchain were developed. The world of Bitcoin continued to grow over the years. Its growth was shown to be exponential as the overall size of the bitcoin blockchain doubled in one year from 2016 to 2017. The term itself, blockchain, was not used until 2016.

As the use of bitcoin spread around the internet, the total number of users who utilized blockchain technology grew. At one point the USD value of Bitcoin was nearly zero. In the span of ten years, the currency went from $0.003 to nearly $20,000. The rapid rise of bitcoin led to an increased trust and popularity in blockchain technology. Just as blockchain was an essential component to the rise of Bitcoin, Bitcoin is integral to the rise of blockchain technology. It is certain we will see more applications of blockchain emerge in the world as the years come. So far, the most obvious application is circumventing financial institutions with digital currency.

The rise of Bitcoin brought with it many similar technologies and imitations. While some new cryptocurrencies were very similar to Bitcoin or other popular alternatives, the most successful new cryptocurrencies sought to solve new problems. Today, there are a great number of new cryptocurrencies. There is no doubt that in the future we will see the total number of cryptocurrencies available continue to grow. Let's take a look at some of the more popular cryptocurrencies that have emerged after Bitcoin: Litecoin and Ethereum. These systems have sprung out of the cryptocurrency market Bitcoin has created, and they offer new features and solutions to the world of cryptocurrency.

Arguably the second most popular cryptocurrency, Litecoin is considered by many to be analogous to silver. Bitcoin, or gold, would be the most popular cryptocurrency with more predictable patterns and investors. Litecoin, or silver, would also be a well-known cryptocurrency, but the market lends itself towards more price fluctuations and a smaller market cap. As the name implies, Litecoin is a lighter version of Bitcoin. It is nearly completely identical to Bitcoin with the exception of a few features. For one, the maximum block-size is smaller. This means transactions can be carried out faster. Another difference is the use of a function called "scrypt." This function is applied in the mining process, and it makes it easier for less powerful computers to mine Litecoin than Bitcoin.

How did Litecoin come to be? The origin of Litecoin is similar to Bitcoin in that it was released as open-source software. The creator of Litecoin was a former Google employee by the name of Charlie Lee. The software was released on October 7, 2011. Litecoin would later go on live on October 13, 2011. Initially, Litecoin was actually a fork of the Bitcoin Core client. The main modifications that were made were a modified interface, the use of scrypt over Bitcoin's hashing algorithm, decreased time to generate blocks, and an increase in the maximum possible number of cryptocoins.

A cryptocurrency that is similar to Bitcoin, but not identical, is Ethereum. Ethereum also ranks itself in the top tier of cryptocurrencies and is nearly as popular as Litecoin. Unlike Litecoin, Ethereum seeks to create a new platform and offer additional features to the cryptocurrency platform. For one, Ethereum is offered as an operating system. Ethereum provides a scripting platform for cryptocurrency applications, allowing many to develop their own cryptocurrency apps and services on top of Ethereum. On top of being an operating system and scripting platform, Ethereum also functions as a normal cryptocurrency like the previously mentioned Bitcoin and Litecoin.

You may be wondering, what are the origins of Ethereum? Initially, Ethereum was outlined in a white paper by a programmer who participated in a print publication called "Bitcoin Magazine" named Vitalik Buterin. His goal was to create a way for people to build decentralized applications. After this announcement in 2013, a development team was assembled in 2014. After funding the project through a public crowdsale of cryptocoin units, Ethereum was launched. A group called the Enterprise Ethereum Alliance was formed and garnered over 116 members, including massive corporations like Microsoft, J.P. Morgan, Intel, and national banks. Ethereum is used today as a development platform and popular cryptocoin for trading and investing.

In 2014, the use of Bitcoin Automatic Teller Machines, or Bitcoin ATM's, began in Austin, Texas. Three years later in 2017, there were over 1,500 Bitcoin ATM's installed across the world. These devices allowed people to physically buy and sell Bitcoins with cash. Usually, a fee was charged for these services in the form of a percentage. In 2017, the average fee of a Bitcoin ATM was roughly 9%. Just like normal bank ATMs, Bitcoin ATMs can be found in various locations such as gas stations, bars, malls, and elsewhere. Businesses who install Bitcoin ATMs on their premises often pull in a good amount of profit.

In review, we have learned the conditions behind the origins of cryptocurrency. We have examined the humble beginnings of the first cryptocurrency, Bitcoin, and the explosive growth that followed immediately after. The recent advent of cryptocurrency technology is certainly unique for its time. In this next chapter, we will look at the many applications of cryptocurrency in the market.

CHAPTER 4
APPLICATIONS OF CRYPTOCURRENCY

There are certainly a great number of applications of cryptocurrency technology. In this chapter, we will explore the many ways that people have found, are finding, and may find the use of cryptocurrency. We will cover cryptocurrency trading, investing, smart contracts, decentralized applications, commerce, wealth management, education, and a couple of ideas for future use of cryptocurrency. There is little doubt that many new applications for cryptocurrency will emerge in the future. The underlying technology behind Bitcoin, blockchain, has already been applied by many different institutions, including governments and global banks. As the number of applications of cryptocurrency grows, the technology will become generally more commonplace and well-known.

To start, what is the difference between trading and investing cryptocurrency? The two applications involve the same initial process but differ in their latter halves. In trading, you are buying an amount of cryptocurrency in the short-term to sell it at a higher price for a profit. In investing, you are buying cryptocurrency to hold onto in the long-term. With both methods, you are seeking to acquire digital currency at a low price and eventually sell it at a higher price for a profit. There are many different tools and exchanges for buying and selling cryptocurrency, but we will go into more detail on this subject in the next chapter.

Trading cryptocurrency is not for the faint of heart. The process involves a lot of research, fundamental analyses, quick thinking, and a wise approach to the psychology of trading. Just like the real-world currency market, the cryptocurrency market is highly volatile. This means that the price is subject to rapid changes over the period of hours or days. As cryptocurrencies are relatively new, it is even more difficult to trade in an already volatile market. Fortunately, there are a number of tried and true strategies for successfully trading cryptocoins. Developers of exchanges and individual traders have made millions and even billions of dollars trading in the cryptocurrency market.

Investing is similar to trading but differs in crucial ways. Investors seek to gain a profit in the long-term by investing capital into cryptocurrencies they believe will generally trend upward over the course of time. This process takes longer than trading but offers the greatest returns and profits. Not only does it take longer for a long-term investment to build value, it also requires more research and fundamental analyses to make it possible. On the positive side, investments do not require constant monitoring and intense trading strategies. A typical investor may only inquire about the status of his investments once or twice a day or even weekly.

Should one trade in cryptocurrency or invest in cryptocurrency? If you are set on trading or investing in cryptocurrency, it is wise to do thorough research beforehand. If you have the time on your hands and a willingness to learn, trading is probably the better route for you. If you have some capital you wish to grow but do not have the time or interested to become an expert in trading cryptocurrency, investing is the wiser choice. Whether you are trading or investing in cryptocurrency, it is important to do proper research and fundamental analyses before making any cryptocurrency market decisions.

Smart contracts are another popular application of cryptocurrency. In a nutshell, a smart contract is a protocol created by a computer that carries out the actions written in a contract automatically. Some applications of smart contracts include the automatic transfer of funds between individuals without the need for a financial institution or third-party. A smart contract could be used to automate the payment of rent, to legally carry out a digital action the precise moment it needs to be carried out, or just to provide a superior alternative to formal contract law. Smart contracts are also an application of blockchain in general.

CRYPTOCURRENCY

Where do smart contracts come from? Smart contracts are another innovation to the world of cryptocurrency that came from Nick Szabo. The phrase emerged on the internet in the year 1996. The term was popularized on a website called Extropy that provided a platform for researchers in computer science and other advanced fields to publish their work and ideas. Nick Szabo published a paper on this website titled, "Smart Contracts: Building Blocks for Digital Free Markets." The paper outlined the basics of smart contracts and how they might be used as the foundation of free markets online. As mentioned earlier, Nick Szabo is also responsible for creating bit gold.

What is a decentralized application? A decentralized application is a type of application that does not require a central server or authority to carry out critical tasks in an application. Decentralized applications are described in the white paper of Ethereum as fitting into three distinct categories. [numbered list] The first is applications that are made to manage money. The second is applications that involve money but also require another asset or unit of value. The last category of decentralized applications is those that do not involve any money. These may include applications that handle voting or the secured storage of critical documents.

The impact of decentralized applications is profound. With cryptocurrencies, the need for financial institutions in the transfer of funds is eliminated. This technology does not seek to disrupt the way financial institutions are run, but instead to lay a new groundwork for finance that excludes financial institutions. However, financial institutions in the transaction of funds are not the only thing rendered obsolete by decentralized applications like cryptocurrencies. Decentralized applications can also be used by governments, activists, and organizations to provide a system of distributed trust and automation. Governments like Russia's are already devising systems for voting that revolve around decentralized applications.

Commerce is one of the most obvious applications of cryptocurrency. By using cryptocurrency instead of fiat currency, or cash, in exchange for goods and services, many benefits are conferred. For one, business done with cryptocurrency is very time and cost-efficient. The customer and the business can work together directly and transfer funds across any distance with minimal fees and no third-parties. Secondly, business done with cryptocurrency is completely private and anonymous. One can buy and sell goods using cryptocurrency without going the process of exchanging personal information for use with financial institutions or groups seeking to profit from one's personal data.

What goods and services can be bought and sold with cryptocurrency? Practically any good you can purchase with cash can also be purchased directly with cryptocurrency. Perhaps most importantly, you can buy and sell fiat currency with cryptocurrency. This includes US Dollars, Euros, Japanese Yen, and any other viable currency. With the right amount of cryptocoins, one can buy flights, hotels, music, apps, retail goods, gold, the services of legal and accounting firms, pizza, university tuition, donations to charities, and practically any other product. Commerce may be the most clear and popular application of cryptocurrency in the market, but it is dwarfed in comparison to all of the other applications.

Wealth management is another facet of the cryptocurrency market. Throughout history, many individuals and families have managed their wealth through investing and trading in valuable assets. A wealth management portfolio may include some assets such as real estate, stocks, bonds, precious metals, and other valuable resources and financial instruments. Cryptocurrency is emerging as another element to be found in the portfolio of services designed to manage wealth. Just as Forex and currency trading are used in wealth management, Bitcoin and cryptocurrency trading are taking hold. In the future, cryptocurrency assets may make up a large portion of an individual's portfolio.

How does wealth management with cryptocurrencies work? Some companies like SwissBorg offer wealth management solutions to investors interested in cryptocurrency. You can invest in tokens that are distributed via blockchain and hold a similar function to other cryptocoins. However, there is also a fund that can be invested in that employs the use of cryptocurrency trading but is not actually integrated into a blockchain system itself. These funds work by using the money invested by customers to trade and invest in Bitcoin and other cryptocoins. There is potential for more wealth management services other than SwissBorg to emerge in the market.

An interesting application of cryptocurrency technology is education. One can use the cryptocurrency they have acquired to purchase an education at various schools. These schools include major universities across the world, but also pre-schools and lower level schools that require tuition. This is an interesting development as cryptocurrencies are not tied to any particular region or nation. One could acquire cryptocurrencies in one nation and spend it on an education in another without ever having to exchange currencies or worry about the difference in fiat currency value. As the technology grows, we will likely see more and more schools accepting cryptocurrency as payment.

What schools, in particular, accept cryptocurrency as payment? One school, in particular, is the Lucerne University of Applied Sciences and Arts in Switzerland. Another business school in Berlin, Germany called ESMT Berlin also accepts cryptocurrencies such as Bitcoin as payments for tuition and other costs. The first school to adopt cryptocurrency payments was the University of Nicosia in Cyprus in 2013. The first school in the US to accept cryptocurrency as proper payment was New York City's King's College in 2014. These schools accept Bitcoin and other cryptocoins in exchange for the same services a student would purchase with fiat currency. Other institutions of education such as Princeton, Yale, and UC Berkeley now offer courses on cryptocurrency for students.

One possible application of cryptocurrency that may develop in the future is crowdfunding. Unlike standard fiat currency, units of cryptocurrency can be divided into very small fractions. A cryptocurrency worth $1,000 per cryptocoin unit can be divided into decimal amounts worth $0.01 each. With this in mind, cryptocurrencies are a good source of crowdfunding. Thousands of users can contribute just a small amount of cryptocoins and fund a project worth hundreds of thousands of dollars. The largest crowdfunded projects are blockchain based. The largest single crowdfunded project, in particular, is Filecoin. Filecoin is a decentralized application that rose a little over $250 million dollars through cryptocurrency crowdfunding.

Lastly, an application of cryptocurrency we will likely see in the future is the expansion of decentralized autonomous organizations. Shortened as DAO, a decentralized autonomous organization serves as an organized, automated group without any one leader. These organizations usually operate on systems that involve a distributed ledger like a cryptocurrency. There are rules set for how members can invest funds and vote on organization decisions, and no one person or group of people control the direction of the DAO. This is useful as boards and chairmen can often make the wrong decision to the detriment of the whole group. With a DAO, everyone involved gets to participate in the voting system and make wise decisions with investments.

What is an example of decentralized autonomous organizations? One such example is Dash. This is a cryptocurrency that was formally known as XCoin or Darkcoin. The governance and budgeting of Dash are completely decentralized among a distributed ledger. Just as cryptocoin units are distributed among the decentralized ledger. Operators of important nodes in the network can vote to distribute a portion of the funds towards projects that benefit Dash. This is useful as individuals who have invested money in the cryptocurrency have a say in how the funds are invested to grow the value of the cryptocurrency.

As you can see, there are numerous applications of cryptocurrencies. We have explored the applications of cryptocurrency trading, investing, smart contracts, decentralized applications, commerce, wealth management, education, and a couple of ideas for future use of cryptocurrency. There are too many applications to list and explain in this book alone, and much more to come in the future. This should provide you with a general idea of cryptocurrency applications. In the following chapter, we will examine the world of cryptocurrency trading and invest in depth.

CHAPTER 5
TRADING AND INVESTING CRYPTOCURRENCY

Trading and investing cryptocurrency is an activity very similar to trading foreign currency on the Forex market, the largest market in the world. Prices are volatile, volumes are large, and investing properly requires a lot of research and foresight. In this chapter, we will cover the basics of cryptocurrency trading and investing, fundamental analysis, exchanges, trading strategies, the investment process, and rudimentary risk management. Trading and investing in cryptocurrency requires startup capital, effort spent in research and analysis, and technological know-how. This chapter should give you a reasonable foundation for the industry, but it is recommended to read further on the subject before approaching this market.

Let's review the main difference between trading and investing. A cryptocurrency trader is looking to make a profit on position on a timespan from anywhere between hours and a couple weeks. Trading involves analyzing trends, buying cryptocoins when they are cheap, and selling them when the price goes up. Per trade, traders make less money than long-term investors but may make more money over time performing several trades in a short time span. What's important to a trader isn't making a huge profit on one big trade, but consistently making a decent profit on many different trades. In general, trading requires more time and effort than simply investing.

A cryptocurrency investor is also looking to make a profit on a cryptocurrency position, but the timespan involved may be a few months to a decade. Investors stand to make the most profit per investment. For example, an investor in Bitcoin could purchase $1 worth of Bitcoin in 2009 and sell it for a profit of $3.4 million USD in 2017. That's a good return on investment that was only possible from holding a long-term position for 8 years and then selling when the time was right. Investing requires more initial research and planning than individual trades, but once the investment is made it requires less attention than trades completed daily or weekly.

Fundamental analysis is the process of determining the health of an investment before committing any money. A good fundamental analysis will tell you whether or not an investment is healthy and worth the potential risk. In the world of cryptocurrency, fundamental analysis is done on up and coming cryptocoins and cryptocoins that have been around a while. A solid strategy for fundamental analysis in the cryptocurrency market is a series of questions that can be used to determine if the price of a cryptocoin will rise in the future. For most positions and trading strategies, you want the price of the cryptocoin to rise over time after investing your initial capital.

Your sources on performing a fundamental analysis are just as important as the questions you need to ask of the cryptocurrency. The first source you should consult is the white papers.

White papers are documents created by the development team of a cryptocoin that details how the coin works and why it was created. Consider these documents to be the primary source of your information on the cryptocurrency. Next, you want to find the main communication channels of the development team of your chosen cryptocoin. This may be on a chat application such as slack, or on their official development blog. By doing this you can keep yourself up to date on all the latest developments of the coin you are investing in. You may even be able to communicate and interact with the developers of the coin. Lastly, you can find good cryptocurrency information you can find is the community forums. We've already covered Bitcoin Forum, but there are other places to find cryptocurrency discussion. If you are active on the internet you may have already heard of the social media website, Reddit. On this website there are pages that serve as forums on many different topics. These pages are called "subreddits." These places are all extremely useful in doing a proper fundamental analysis of a cryptocoin.

CRYPTOCURRENCY

Where can you find white papers? Usually, a simple google search will yield good results. The more popular the coin the easier it is to find the white papers. For example, Bitcoin's white papers can be found on their primary website by navigating through the side menus. It shouldn't be too hard to find these papers for any relatively popular coin. If you are having difficulty finding the white papers for an obscure coin, try finding a way to contact the development team. If you express your interests politely, they may share the documents with you. Again, don't invest in a cryptocoin without first reading the white papers. This is like the bible of the cryptocurrency.

Where can you find the development blog or slack chat? Like the white papers, a simple Google search can do the trick. More reputable coins like Bitcoins have large communities and high-profile updates from developers. As of right now, you can request an invitation to the Bitcoin development slack chat at https://bitcoincoreslack.herokuapp.com/. The development blog is also available on their main .org domain. For more obscure cryptocoins you can find their blog and slack chat through search engines. As with the white papers, the more popular the cryptocurrency is the easier it will connect yourself with the community and developers.

Where can I find these community forums? By searching on Google you can likely find a subreddit for your chosen cryptocurrency as well as discussion forums on other sites like Steemit. For example, the official bitcoin subreddit can be found at this address: https://www.reddit.com/r/Bitcoin/. Reddit also has a built-in search function for finding subreddits on the sidebar of their website. Steemit is a similar site that pays users for submitting and curating content. There is a lot of information for cryptocurrency investing on this site. It's sort of like Reddit, but it uses money instead of upvotes and downvotes.

Once you've gathered your sources, you can begin performing your fundamental analysis. Here are a series of questions you should ask yourself before considering investing or trading any particular cryptocurrency.

CRYPTOCURRENCY

How different is the coin from the nearest competitor? One sign of a quality cryptocoin is whether or not it is original in its approach. If the cryptocurrency you are analyzing is essentially a copy of another coin with a different label, it will not have as much promise at increasing in value in the future. You want to invest in a cryptocoin that aims to solve new problems and create value in an innovative way. In a way, this is similar to analyzing a company. Does this cryptocoin offer something new to the market that doesn't exist already?

How is the coin supplied? To understand how the price of the cryptocurrency will change, you have to understand how the coins are brought into the market. For Bitcoin, new coins are introduced into the market through mining. Some other coins are issued through using a website or performing a particular action. Following the law of supply and demand, if the supply of a coin decreases at some point it should increase value for investors. Ensure that there is a consistent manner in which coins are created and brought to the market. This method could be centralized or decentralized, but it must be reliable and consistent.

Are the creators of the coin experienced developers? The main team that makes up the developers of the coin is critical to determining the success, and therefore profitability, of investing in the coin. If the development team is experienced and has a good track record, this is a solid indicator that the coin is worth investing in. If the team behind the cryptocurrency doesn't seem to have a good track record, think twice before investing. Creating a new cryptocurrency is like starting a business. The more experienced the founders are, the more likely it is that the cryptocoin will succeed.

What is the target demographic? Cryptocurrencies are aimed at serving a particular demographic. It's crucial that the cryptocoin you are looking at has a sizable target demographic that is clear and easy to define. With a high number of people willing to participate in the cryptocurrency, it is likely that it will grow and become a lucrative investment. Using the Bitcoin example again, the main target demographic developers had in mind was people who wanted to move money without the aid of financial institutions. A good prospect of capturing a large share of the market is a good indicator of a quality cryptocurrency.

If you can find promising answers to these questions, the cryptocoin you have in mind is a good decision. First, ensure the cryptocoin is unique in approach and the problem that it solves. Next, figure out how new coins are brought into the market and what this means for the future of the value of the cryptocoin. If you can perform a good fundamental analysis on your coin of choice, you can make a good profitable position on your chosen cryptocoin.

Cryptocurrency exchanges are places where you can buy, sell, and exchange various cryptocurrencies. You can exchange fiat currency (cash) for cryptocoins, trade one type of coin for another, and sell your coins back into fiat. The first exchange we'll explain is Coinbase. Coinbase is a very popular exchange that has been mentioned by The Wall Street Journal and the New York Times. It charges a flat fee for transactions under $200 (USD) and percentage fee depending on your region. GDAX is another reputable exchange. It is back by the New York Stock Exchange and is federally insured by the

United States government. It offers a 0% fee on high-frequency traders and fees as low as 0.1%. GDAX is owned by the same corporation that runs Coinbase. Bittrex is an exchange based in the USA that supports algorithmic trading. Algorithmic trading is a technique that involves using code and programmed bots to buy and sell cryptocurrency. This exchange charges a transaction fee of 025%. Bittrex features a large variety of different cryptocoins. There are many other exchanges not mentioned here that you can easily find with an online search.

With your chosen exchange, now is the time to research your investment strategy. It makes sense to start with the most straight-forward of trading strategies: Long-position trading. As the name implies, long-position trading is buying in and holding on for an extended period of time. This kind of investment is referred to as a passive investment strategy. With long-position trading, you buy some cryptocurrency and hold onto for weeks, years, possibly even a decade or longer. The next category of strategies is naturally day trading strategies. Again, as the name implies, day trading is buying and selling cryptocurrencies within the span of a day. These positions do not last as long but allow you to make money on a day-to-day basis.

To begin your first foray into cryptocurrency trading you need to buy primary coins on an exchange such as the ones mentioned earlier. Create an account with your chosen exchange. After creating your account walk through the provided steps to buy primary coins such as Bitcoin. Once you see the value of your primary coin increase by the amount you want, it's time to sell your secondary coin back into primary coin and cash out. This process is essentially the investment process detailed earlier but in reverse. Calculate any fees you might have to pay for these transactions in your initial planning.

These are core concepts behind buying and selling cryptocoins. Consider this to be a primer or skeleton of investing and trading in cryptocurrency. We cannot cover absolutely everything you need to know in one chapter on cryptocurrency trading and investing, but this should give you an idea of what you should be researching. In this next chapter, we will take a look at some of the legal concerns behind cryptocurrency.

CHAPTER 6
LEGAL CONCERNS

As cryptocurrency is a new and emerging technology, new laws are being created to handle cryptocurrency. In this chapter, we will cover cryptocurrency taxes, regulations, monetary policy, ICOs, the SAFT, money laundering, corruption enabling and prevention, and risk of litigation. There are many new laws surrounding cryptocurrency, and more coming each day. In general, governments want in on all of the revenue being generated by cryptocurrency, but the decentralized nature of the system makes this difficult. With these new laws, rules are outlined for how cryptocurrency is taxed, how cryptocurrency is regulated by governments and potential new laws for requiring the release of information on cryptocurrency assets.

With individuals and groups making large amounts of figures buying and selling cryptocurrency, many are basing some or all of their income on cryptocurrency earning and businesses. As a result of this, there are laws on taxing earnings made from trading cryptocurrency. There is one main case in which your earnings on cryptocurrency are taxable. This case is called a "taxable event." The main taxable event for cryptocurrency is when you sell your cryptocoins for fiat currency. This is the last process in cryptocurrency trading and investing when your cryptocurrency assets become liquid and spendable as government-issued fiat currency.

There are other taxable events in the world of cryptocurrency. You are not only taxed when your cryptocurrency is sold for fiat currency, but taxable events occur when one type of cryptocurrency is exchanged for another or when cryptocurrency is used to pay for goods or services. These taxable events are the same when applied to fiat currency. If you purchase one type of cryptocurrency using another, you will have to pay taxes on that transaction. If you accept cryptocurrency in exchange for providing a good or service, you will also have to pay taxes on that. These are the situations in which an individual or business will have to pay taxes on cryptocurrency.

On top of taxes, the government provides regulations for the cryptocurrency market. One source of such regulations in the US is the Securities and Exchange Commission or SEC. This organization is responsible for the regulation of the sales of securities and other financial instruments and assets. In July 2017, the Securities Exchange Commission issued a bulletin on cryptocurrency fundraising events called ICOs, or Initial Coin Offerings. They said that they can be fair and lawful investment opportunities but has created three actions of enforcement to use against sponsors of ICOs. The first of which was a halt and exposure of an alleged fraud. The second was a similar case of halt and exposure to a fraud. The last and third action was a statement of concern about participants in the market who extended customer credit in the same nation.

Another such regulatory agency that has decided to impose regulations on the cryptocurrency market is the Commodity Futures Trading Commission or CFTC. This organization has declared Bitcoin as a normal commodity to be under the same laws and regulations as other commodities. This means that anyone attempting to commit fraud while using Bitcoin as a commodity is subject to the same lawful punishments as someone attempting to commit fraud for any other commodity. They also allowed financial institutions like the CME and CBOE to issue futures on Bitcoins. It approved a platform from a corporation called LedgerX, LLC that provided derivatives clearing and swaps execution.

When it comes to fiat currency, the federal government has the final say in how much money is printed and where it is coming from. In the case of the US government, US dollars are issued by mints according to the federal government's ideas of how the value of the currency is moving and how to maintain financial health. When it comes to cryptocurrency, the issuing of cryptocoins is outside of the hands of the federal government. In fact, one does not even need a third-party financial institution to create and transacts units of cryptocoins. Let's look at the way monetary policy affects cryptocurrency in our current times.

At the moment, the amount of cryptocurrency in the market is not enough to influence the monetary policy of the US government's main bank, the Federal Reserve. In the future, there may be enough value in circulation in the form of cryptocurrency that it will affect the policies of the Federal Reserve. The Federal Reserve does not see cryptocurrency as a threat to the state of monetary policy, but in fact, considers is a potential gain for the economy overall. Even if the cryptocurrency market did affect monetary policy for any particular federal government in any nation, there is nothing any government could do to regulate the creation and distribution of cryptocoins.

An ICO, as mentioned earlier, is short for Initial Coin Offering. How exactly do Initial Coin Offerings work? The term ICO is based on the term IPO or Initial Public Offering. An Initial Public Offering is a term used to describe the emergence of a new corporation on the stock market. An Initial Public Offering is an important event for a new corporation. During this event, people on the inside of the corporation who holds a large stake in the company often sell their shares the moment the company goes public. This results in a large profit and usually causes the price to decrease.

An Initial Coin Offering is somewhat different. An Initial Coin Offering occurs before a new cryptocoin is even offered for purchase and sale on an exchange. The idea of an Initial Coin Offering is to provide an opportunity for investors to get in on a new cryptocoin before it is made available to the public. The idea is units of the cryptocoin are sold to investors for large sums of money before the coin goes public, and then the investors sell their shares after the coin has gone public and appreciated in value. However, not all Initial Coin Offerings are good investments, hence the need for fundamental analysis as mentioned earlier in the book.

Another type of investment instrument in the legal regulation of cryptocoins is called a Simple Agreement for Future Tokens, or SAFT. The format of the Simple Agreement for Future Tokens is particularly appealing to a class of investors known as venture capitalist. A venture capitalist is an individual who buys and sells business and financial instruments like cryptocoins to generate a profit. A Simple Agreement for Future Tokens appeals to venture capitalists as it provides an opportunity to invest in a new and promising technology and potentially net a large profit after initial costs.

But what is a Simple Agreement for Future Tokens and how exactly does it work? In a Simple Agreement for Future Tokens deal, a venture capitalist will invest a specific amount of fiat currency in a new startup and the developers and managers of the new cryptocoin will promise to give them a specific amount of tokens that it is selling in an Initial Coin Offering. The idea of a Simple Agreement for Future Tokens is that after the cryptocoin has completed the Initial Coin Offering and is operating in businesses and exchanges, the cryptocoins will become more valuable and thus profitable to sell.

Another legal concern when it comes to the cryptocurrency market is the risk of people using cryptocoins for money laundering. What is money laundering? When an individual or group acquires any amount of currency, it is considered income in the eyes of the government. If the money was acquired illegally, the government still wants a cut of the income in the form of taxes. However, illegal funds can be traced back to illegal activities and lead to the arrest and incarceration of the criminals involved. To give the government their cut of the profits and stay out of legal trouble, the money is moved through legitimate businesses that pay taxes for the government. In the USA money laundering was made illegal, but not until the year 1986.

How can cryptocurrency become involved in money laundering? For one, it is impossible to tie cryptocoin ownership and transactions to any one individual or group if the information is not volunteered. This makes it very difficult and plain impossible in many cases to track where and how much money is moving through the cryptocurrency market. This makes cryptocurrencies an easy target for individuals seeking to launder money. Surprisingly enough, cases for money laundering that involve cryptocurrency are minuscule and nearly negligible compared to all the other tried cases for money laundering. Japan, the nation that has seen the most cases of cryptocurrency money laundering, has reported that only 0.17% of money laundering cases involve cryptocurrency in any way.

It's not a surprise that a system that allows anyone to transfer any amount of money anonymously, securely, and instantly is not involved in corruption. The potential for cryptocurrency to be abused in the form of bribing government officials is huge. A corporation, individual, or criminal group can send any amount of funds to a senator, bureaucrat, legislator, or even world leader in exchange for political favors. This circumvents the need for special interest groups to bribe legislators for laws that protect their corporation or special interest. The potential for corruption through the use of cryptocoins is alarmingly great.

Fortunately, the technology behind cryptocurrency can and is currently being used to battle corruption. The main technology that cryptocurrency operates on, the blockchain, is particularly powerful in preventing corruption. In the distributed transaction ledger of cryptocurrencies like Bitcoin, the transaction data is timestamped and irreversible without solving the cryptographic hash that secures it. This means blockchain technology can be used to secure any sort of government or official document from modification. The government of India is already using blockchain to secure land documents and prevent the hundreds of millions of dollars being spent to bribe government officials into changing the documents in the land registry and committing land fraud.

With certain uses of cryptocoins, there comes the risk of litigation. Litigation involving cryptocurrency only occurs if something goes wrong. This means breaching contracts and lying about cryptocoins for a profit in the form of fraud. As more and more people employ the use of cryptocurrency, more and more laws and potential cases for litigation involving the technology will appear. One case in which litigation would be required for the use of cryptocurrency is the breach of a contract of an Initial Coin Offering or Simple Agreement of Future Tokens. If one party fails to pay the required funds for the cryptocoins, or the other party fails to provide said cryptocoins, they are vulnerable to legal action forcing the extraction of said funds.

Another case in which litigation could occur in the world of cryptocurrency is fraud. Unfortunately, every legitimate business comes with it individuals or groups that seek to lie to investors, customers, or founders and turn a profit. If a cryptocoin is created or proposed and then completely neglects to meet the promised proposals, the group or individual involved in the fraud is subject to litigation. Of course, parties affected by fraud can choose not to press charges, but in many cases, it is wise to take an organization who commits fraud against you to court. These are the two main cases in which the cryptocurrency market may involve litigation.

In review, there are a good number of legal matters involved cryptocurrency and cryptocoin trading and investing. As the technology grows and is adopted by an increasing number of citizens and governments, laws surrounding cryptocurrency will also grow. The main legal matters surrounding cryptocurrency are cryptocurrency taxes, regulations, monetary policy, ICOs, the SAFT, money laundering, corruption enabling and prevention, and risk of litigation. In general, if you are conducting business in the realm of cryptocurrency and cryptocoins in a thoughtful and lawful manner, you will not run into any litigation or legal concerns. However, it is wise to research all the laws and potential financial opportunities provided by cryptocurrency law.

CHAPTER 7
SECURITY RISKS

Much like the dotcom boom or any new and exciting market, there are bound to be some who seek to lie or commit fraud in the realm of cryptocurrency. This is a hard fact of business. Also, trading and investing in cryptocurrency does not come without risk. Fortunately, knowing how to identify a healthy cryptocurrency investment and how to mitigate risk when investing and trading will minimize any potential losses you may incur. As we have already covered how to do a proper fundamental analysis and identify a good cryptocoin investment from a bad one, this chapter will mainly cover strategies you can employ in managing risk while trading and investing in cryptocurrency.

Risk management is an essential tool for any successful investor or trader in cryptocurrency. Risk management means controlling any possible losses so you don't lose too much if things go wrong. Even if your trading strategies and analysis are golden, without a good risk management strategy you stand to lose more money than you have to. Good risk management will ease your mind and minimize any potential losses you may have. Read these strategies carefully and apply them to your trading and investing. In this chapter, we'll cover several different risk management strategies and how to apply them to your cryptocurrency trading and investing.

The first of these strategies is dollar cost averaging. Dollar cost averaging, or DCA is a technique that involves buying a specific fiat currency amount of an investment on a periodic basis over a specified period of time. This means you are buying your investment piece by piece over time instead of all at once in a lump sum. This can be done on a monthly, weekly, or even daily basis. By spreading your investment over a longer period of time, you reduce the risk of the price changing unfavorably immediately after making the investment all at once. Let's look at an example of dollar cost averaging applied to cryptocurrency.

Let's say you want to invest $1000 into Bitcoin, and that Bitcoin is generally trending upwards. You can invest all $1000 at once, or you can use dollar cost averaging and invest $100 per month until you've invested $1000 total. As we learned earlier, even a general uptrend will have swings upwards and downwards. If you invested $1000 all at once, and the price swings downwards, your position is not profitable. If you invest it piece by piece over 10 months and the trend continues upwards, you make an overall profit that is fundamentally less risky.

The next strategy we'll learn is buying the dip. In market terms, buying the dip means buying in directly after the price has declined. Prices in the cryptocurrency market will follow general trends but correct itself around the mean. Nobody can predict the market completely, but you can expect the price of a cryptocoin to correct itself upwards after a dip below the mean price. The difficult part of this strategy is predicting when the dip is over and the movement of the price will reverse itself. If you buy in a dip that is actually the beginning of a downtrend, you stand to lose a profitable position. Let's look at another example, this time an application of buying the dip to the cryptocurrency market.

You have been eyeing a cryptocurrency that seems healthy after a thorough fundamental analysis. The general trend of this cryptocurrency price is upwards. One day, you see the price dip below the average price. This means that the price will soon correct itself and maintain the overall upward trend. If you buy into the cryptocoin now you will likely see the price correct itself and go upwards. If you were to buy into the cryptocurrency on the upward swing before the dip, your investment would lose money when the dip occurred. Watch the movement of your cryptocoin closely to see when the dip begins to correct itself. It's better to see evidence of the correction beginning than betting on it before it happens.

The following risk management strategy you might have heard mentioned in pop culture or elsewhere. It is called diversifying your portfolio.

CRYPTOCURRENCY

Diversifying your portfolio means spreading your investment capital over several different opportunities. As the old saying goes, never put all your eggs in one basket. By putting all of your investment capital into one position you risk losing all of your capital in one fell swoop. By properly diversifying your portfolio, or your overall collection of investments and trades, you reduce the total amount of money you can lose. If one investment goes sour, you still have all the others to keep you afloat.

How can you apply diversifying your portfolio to cryptocurrency? Imagine you have $10,000 to invest in cryptocurrency. If you were to put it all into one cryptocurrency you stand to lose your entire investment. If you were to invest it in ten different cryptocurrencies you manage your risk. This requires more effort but pays off. Even if two of the cryptocoins you invested in dropped in price, you would still have eight other cryptocoins to profit from. No investment or trade is a sure-fire bet, and by diversifying your portfolio you greatly mitigate any potential losses you may incur.

Following diversifying your portfolio, balancing your portfolio is just as important. Balancing your portfolio involves choosing the investments that are right for you and your situation. If you have a lot of time and reasonable capital to invest, you can benefit from being more aggressive in balancing your portfolio. If you are nearing retirement or winding up your cryptocurrency trading and investing days, you should be more cautious with your portfolio. Understand your current situation and what you stand to lose to properly balance your portfolio. An unbalanced portfolio leads to unnecessary risks as well as missing out on potential profits.

In cryptocurrency balancing your portfolio means choosing the cryptocoins that are right for your situation. If you plan on having a lot of time in your life to buy and sell cryptocurrency, it pays to take a little more risk in composing your portfolio. If you are around the age of retirement and need solid investments that give a consistent return, it pays to be more cautious when choosing your cryptocoins. In general, cryptocoins that have been around a long time and show clear trends are the safer bet. Cryptocoins that are very new or have not even launched yet are riskier, but you stand to make a greater return.

One technique you can employ in risk management is locking in your profits. This means selling off part of your investment to ensure a profit even if the price plummets. Another word for locking in your profits is realization. Remember, you have not made a profit on your position until you actually sell it and close your position. By locking in your profits you guarantee that no matter what happens your investment will make a profit. By leaving part of your investment in the position, you also stand to gain even more if the price moved favorably. Let's look at an example of locking in your profits in cryptocurrency.

Let's imagine the price of Bitcoin is $100. You buy five Bitcoins for a total price of $500. Later on, the price of Bitcoin rises to $1,000. You sell two of your bitcoins for $2,000 and lock in a profit of $1,500. No matter how the price of Bitcoin moves after this, you have guaranteed a profit by covering your initial cost of $500 and profiting $1,500. There's no fool-proof way of predicting exactly how the price will move in the future, but you have ensured a profit from your investment while still holding onto the majority of it. Locking in your profits is a very powerful tool for risk management.

To prevent any losses further than what you've planned, you can utilize what is called a stop-loss order. A stop-loss order is a tool that automatically sells your position after it has reached or fallen below a specific price. By holding onto an investment that experiences a major price drop, you end up losing a lot of potential profit and ultimately your initial investment. With a stop-loss order, your investment is sold before it gets any lower and you hold onto most of your initial capital. Remember to do your research well before employing a stop-loss order in your investment. This can backfire if the price drops below your stop-loss order and then swings back up higher than it was before.

A good example of a stop-loss order in cryptocurrency would be setting a price on a secondary coin at which you automatically sell. Many exchanges offer this option and it would be wise to make good use of it. Keep in mind the cryptocurrency market is volatile and a price drop may soon correct itself, leading to the loss of a potential profit opportunity. Let's say you purchase $1,000 worth of Bitcoin at a price of $100 each. You put in a stop-loss order at $80 per Bitcoin. The next day, the price drops to $50. Your stop-loss order would activate when the price dropped to $80. While you would end up losing $200, but without the stop-loss order, you would lose $500.

Much like stop-loss orders, limit orders are used to sell your position at a specific price. Unlike stop-loss orders, you can also use a limit order to buy a position at a specific price. You can refer to a limit order to buy at a specific price as a buy limit order. Vice-versa, you can refer to a limit order to sell at a specific price as a sell limit order. Limit orders allow you to be extremely precise with your trades and investments, guaranteeing specific amounts of profits and minimizing your losses. As long as the market moves as you predict, limit orders can be very useful.

Using Bitcoin again as our example, let's imagine a situation in which limit orders would be useful. The price of Bitcoin is $100, and you expect it to move to $200 within the week. Instead of waiting for the exact moment it starts to move upward, you put in a buy limit order for ten coins when Bitcoin hits $110. Next, you put in a sell limit order for ten coins when Bitcoin hits $190. If the market moves as you predicted, you stand to make exactly $800 no matter where the price goes after it reaches $190. Combine this strategy with locking in profits to automatically guarantee your profit on a position and still stay in the market.

The last risk management strategy we'll look at is storing cryptocurrency in cold storage. Much like food products, storing your cryptocurrency in cold storage ensures that it lasts for a long time. Storing your cryptocoins in cold storage involves owning the keys and storing them on your own machine on your own digital wallet. This means using a desktop coin wallet to store your assets. When your cryptocoins are on an exchange or online wallet, you are at risk of losing them. By minimizing the amount of time your cryptocoins are not in cold storage, you minimize the risk of losing them.

CRYPTOCURRENCY

Now that you understand how to do a proper fundamental analysis and mitigate risks, you can avoid and reduce the severity of any losses you may experience. It is a simple reality of cryptocurrency and any other mode of trading and investment that not all investments are good and nothing is without risk. However, with risk comes reward. In review, we have covered a myriad of risk management strategies and how to employ them in your approach to cryptocurrency. It's important to employ these strategies in any and all potential ventures you make into the world of cryptocurrency and cryptocoin trading and investing.

ALFORD BENSON

CONCLUSION

Thank you for making it through to the end of this book. We hope it was informative and able to provide you with all of the tools you need to achieve your goals in the world of cryptocurrency. There is certainly a wide breadth of information and topics surrounding cryptocurrency, and there is still more to learn for the curious. This book should provide you with a good foundation and starting point to get deeper into the world of cryptocurrency. Whether you are an investor, developer, trader, writer, or journalist we hope you have used this book to gain a good foundational understanding of cryptocurrency.

Let us review all of the topics we have covered in this text. The topics we have covered include defining the invention of cryptocurrency, explaining the underlying mechanics behind cryptocurrency, exploring the history of cryptocurrency, reviewing all the new and upcoming applications of the technology, a primer on getting involved with trading and investing cryptocoins, legal concerns facing cryptocurrency, and lastly the security risks involved with cryptocurrency. These topics contain the main ideas behind cryptocurrency. With a reasonably robust understanding of these topics, you can take yourself further into this new and exciting technology.

This has been a thorough and formal guide to cryptocurrency. You can use this text in the future as a reference or simply a refresher if you choose to delve deeper into cryptocurrency and cryptocoin trading and investing. Finally, if you found this book useful in any way, a review on Amazon is always appreciated!

www.ingramcontent.com/pod-product-compliance
Lightning Source LLC
Chambersburg PA
CBHW051532240526
45471CB00019B/740